I hope you find
deep personal meaning
in this facsimile autograph.

Sincerely,

Ashleigh
Brilliant

I Feel Much Better, Now That I've Given Up Hope©

and *Still More* *BRILLIANT THOUGHTS*®

By *Ashleigh Brilliant*

Woodbridge Press/Santa Barbara, California

1991

Published by
Woodbridge Press Publishing Company
Post Office Box 6189
Santa Barbara, California 93160

Distributed simultaneously in the United States and Canada.

Printed in the United States of America.

Library of Congress Cataloging-in-Publication Data

Brilliant, Ashleigh, 1933-
  I feel much better, now that I've given up hope.

1. Epigrams, American. 2. American wit and humor, pictorial. I. Title.

PN6281.B667   1983   818′k.5402   84-2284
ISBN 0-88007-145-1
ISBN 0-88007-147-8 (soft)

10 9 8 7 6 5

Dedication

*This book
is dedicated to
what most authorities
seem to agree
is a fundamental requirement
for good health:*

Staying Alive.

By Ashleigh Brilliant

Epigrams:

I May Not Be Totally Perfect, but Parts of Me Are Excellent (Santa Barbara, 1979).

I Have Abandoned My Search for Truth, and Am Now Looking for a Good Fantasy (Santa Barbara, 1980).

Appreciate Me Now, and Avoid the Rush (Santa Barbara, 1981).

I Feel Much Better, Now That I've Given Up Hope (Santa Barbara, 1984).

Songs:

The MyGodyssey, It's A Ryndam Shame, and *Seven Seapage* (collections published on board the Floating University, 1965-67).

The Haight-Ashbury Songbook (San Francisco, 1967).

Ashleigh Brilliant in the Haight-Ashbury (LP record album, San Francisco, 1967).

Forward, Australia (proposed new Australian National Anthem, Perth, 1972).

Journalism:

Nine Weeks Across America (in Edgware and District *Post,* London, July-Sept. 1951).

Trash From Ash (column in Haight-Ashbury *Record,* San Francisco, 1967-68).

History:

Prohibition and Contempt for the Law (Berkeley, 1960).

Abolition in Action, 1861-65 (Berkeley, 1961).

Social Effects of the Automobile in Southern California During the 1920's (Berkeley, 1964).

A Brief History of the Seven Seas Division of Chapman College (Orange, California, 1966).

Poetry:

"The Atheist's Prayer" and Other Poems (Los Angeles, 1958).

Unpoemed Titles (Bend, Oregon, 1965).

Criticism:

Housman and the Hangman (Berkeley, 1961).

Drama:

Begetting (a play), (Dorland Mountain Colony, California, 1980).

Contents (and Discontents)

Introduction

First Things Forced

Welcome! (or, if more appropriate, Welcome Back!) In case you don't know where you are, you are in my fourth book of illustrated epigrams, which (whatever you may think of them) I have every right to call Brilliant Thoughts, since Ashleigh Brilliant (whatever you may think of me) is my real name. They are also widely known as *Pot-Shots,* and, since 1967, when they began as postcards, I've been firing them off in a variety of forms and directions, and making quite a game (as well as a living) out of it.

This game has some very challenging rules. All *Pot-Shots* must be: (a) seventeen words or less, (b) easily translatable, (c) intelligible—and (let us hope) enjoyable—even without any illustration, (d) as different as possible from each other (a requirement which, with several thousand now begotten, has at last driven me to a computer), (e) entirely original, individually copyrighted, and, whenever necessary, legally defended against infringement, (f) numbered, catalogued, kept in print on postcards, and made readily available by mail to anybody anywhere in the world. (For details on this extraordinary service, see last page.)

Not What It Themes To Be

My Publisher, for reasons of his own, felt that this book, unlike its three predecessors, should have a "Theme"—and so, officially, the theme is Health. But I haven't taken this too seriously, and you are certainly not obliged to; and if, for any reason, you prefer themelessness, or are personally pained or offended by either Physical or Mental Health, just try to forget you ever saw this paragraph, and you'll hardly feel a thing.

Here's Looking at You

You may think I know nothing about you, but I do know one thing for certain: that at some moment after I write these words, you are reading them, or having them read to you. This in itself enables me to make some interesting deductions about you. For one thing, you obviously understand some language. I can also be fairly sure that, at this reading moment of yours, you are not (or at least not entirely) asleep, and probably not engaged in mortal physical combat or making passionate love. I presume, however, that you are a living member of what we currently call the Human Species (if by chance you are not, please accept my apologies—or my congratulations)—and your mastery of at least one language makes me suspect that you have had some contact with other human beings—which means (for better or worse) that I am probably not the first person who has ever tried to communicate with you. But I further presume that, unless you are a censor or a critic getting paid for doing this, or being forced to do it by some peculiar kind of sadist or some fanatical Ashleigh Brilliant enthusiast, your act of reading is more or less voluntary. Considering how many other things may want, need, and even deserve your attention, allow me to rejoice in being your current choice.

Of Me I Sing

Now that I know something about you, I feel a little more comfortable telling you something about me. One of the very few things about me that will never change (at least, not until they change the calendar) is my date of birth: December 9, 1933. My *place* of birth, however, has already changed. At the time of that earth-shaking advent, the Ashleigh Brilliant Birth place was called the Caerthillian Nursing Home. Located in northwest London, it was a small, private institution where people went to be born. The shock of this event was so great that I was speechless for some time afterwards, and never re-visited the spot until 1971. When I did, I was surprised to find that the same building, as though anticipating my possible future need, had now changed itself into an Old People's Home. They haven't yet (to my knowledge) put up a plaque or a statue to me, but, if you wish to make a pilgrimage, and see what's there now, the address is: 87 Fordwych Road, London N.W.2, England.

After having been born, I wasted a lot of time (some spent professing in the jungles of Academia) before the next major occurrence in my life. It was on February 27, 1967, that I arrived in the Haight-Ashbury district of San Francisco, just in time to make my own contribution to that sensational scene as an impromptu orator and entertainer in Golden Gate Park, near the Haight Street entrance. There, if anyplace, is where my statue really belongs, standing on a milk-crate, holding a small portable microphone, addressing a motley assemblage of other friendly and curious statues recumbent on the grass. Sprinkled among the mindfuls of enlightenment I broadcast from that pulpit were the germs of the Brilliant Thoughts you now find displayed here and on everything from walls and doors to bumpers and bosoms.

Look for me next in Western Australia, a country almost totally unknown to the outside world until, in the course of seeking a new route from my past to my future, I discovered it in 1972. So much did I like what I found there that I acquired a piece of it too big to take home with me. That piece, which came complete with ocean views and kangaroos, stands on the south coast, on a prominence called Torbay Hill, near the beautiful old harbor town of Albany. It would be ideal for the colony of purposeful thinkers I intend to found someday—as soon as I can think of a purpose for it.

We now whisk you to the United States Federal Courthouse

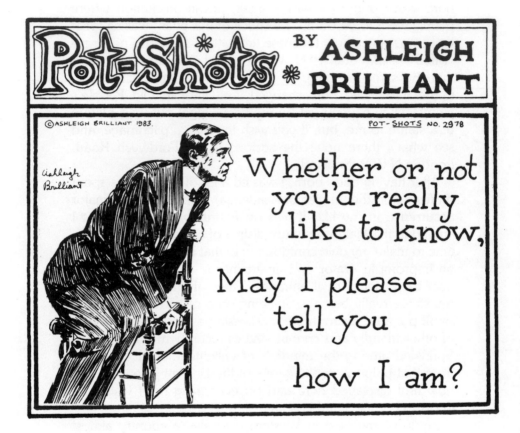

in downtown Los Angeles. The date is September 18, 1979, and, for the first time in my life, I am sitting in a witness-box. The courtroom is hushed; (mainly, I must admit, because it is nearly empty). I am giving testimony in my own behalf in what is to become the famous copyright infringement case of Ashleigh Brilliant v. W.B. Productions, Inc. I am accusing W.B. Productions of pirating several of my epigrams in the form of T-shirt transfers, including one of my best-known Brilliant Thoughts, and the title of my first book, "I MAY NOT BE TOTALLY PERFECT, BUT PARTS OF ME ARE EXCELLENT." The Judge does not seem very friendly. He notices that the book in question contains an Introductory Note by the eminent critic, Clifton Fadiman, and asks me sharply, "Did you pay him to write this?" I assure him that Mr. Fadiman's lukewarm praise was entirely gratis. I am then asked to tell just how I came to write that famous line of which I claim to be the original author. I explain how I was inspired by a celebrated old cartoon by George Du Maurier, first published in *Punch* magazine (November 9, 1895), in which a young curate, dining at the table of his bishop and anxious not to offend him, is asked if he has been given a bad egg. "Oh no, My Lord," he replies, "I assure you—parts of it are excellent." The Judge proves, after all, to be a good egg. He retires to his chambers with my book, and, after several eternities, emerges with an epoch-making decision which penalizes W. B. Productions to the tune of $18,000, and, even more importantly, for the first time clearly establishes that original works such as mine, even though very short, are fully entitled to the protection of the copyright laws. Once again, justice has triumphed over piracy on the high ©'s.

The scene now shifts to a boardroom in Kansas City, Missouri, where a new victory for Ultra-Short Writing is about to be won. We are in the imposing corporate headquarters of the World's Largest and Most Respected Greeting-Card Company, a firm whose policy (like that of most firms in this Industry), when dealing with outside writers of verses and expressions, has always been to buy their little compositions outright, for a single modest fee. The date is November 10, 1982, and, on this historic occasion, the Company's representatives, desiring the right to use the epigrams of Ashleigh Brilliant on certain specified products, and knowing there is only one way to secure it, decide to abandon all precedent, and sign a Royalty Agreement! As if that were not sufficiently astounding, they further agree to the payment of an unheard-of nonrefundable advance of $15,000. Hearing the news, professional epigrammatists all over the world hold mass demonstrations of joy.

Come, finally, to a trail in the hills above Santa Barbara, California (my home since 1973) where, on most mornings, you will find me jogging, my radio head-set tuned to the news, my pockets packed with a survival-kit of pen and paper, to enable any thoughts I might have to survive the journey back down to the little house on West Valerio Street, where, by a magic process called Very Hard Work, they will be transformed into illustrated messages, and eventually distributed far and wide to a desperately needy world.

Unortho Docs

One other thing you should know about me is that officially I am a doctor—a "Doctor of Philosophy," that is. (Berkeley, 1964.) But please don't bring me your ailing philosophies. If my printed messages can't cure them, they are probably beyond all aid. Besides, my Ph.D. is actually in the field of History, and no respectable historian makes any claim to cure anything, not even sick histories.

There are, however, actual medical practitioners who, to my surprise, have been recommending my work to their patients as if it had real medicinal value; and I have even found myself being invited to speak at gatherings of various kinds of Health Professionals and Amateurs, as if seeing me in the flesh could further motivate them to go out and heal. At one of these conventions, one of my fellow featured speakers was Norman Cousins, whose claims that deliberately-induced laughter helped cure him of a serious illness have been widely publicized. Such reports prompted one M.D., Dr. William Goldwag, the author of a syndicated feature called "Ask The Doctor" (Copley News Service), to devote one of his columns to my work under the heading, "The Healing Power of Laughter," and virtually prescribe it as a form of therapy. Brilliant Thoughts, declared Dr. Goldwag, could "be of great help in the healing art . . . contribute materially to your well-being . . . stimulate those healing forces within you to work their magic power." Indeed, "Ashleigh Brilliant may be keeping more people healthy than I am."

All of this was slightly abashing to a very serious and humble author like myself, who has never aspired to anything higher than the Nobel Prize for Literature, and had never even given a thought to the Nobel Prize for Medicine. It has of course been gratifying to be medically sanctioned as not only harmless but positively beneficial—a classification which many equally legitimate new medications have to struggle long and hard to attain. But for me, the experience is something like being for years a dedicated violinist, and then suddenly becoming a celebrity because it's discovered that my music happens to repel insects.

Being of service to the medical community was not, however, an entirely new experience for me. In fact, it recalls the one occasion in my life when I was able to do something truly heroic. The year was 1956, and I was a student at (what was then called) Los Angeles State College, taking courses which would qualify me to become a California High School teacher. One of these courses was in "Audio-Visual Education," and it included learning how to operate a film-projector. In order to demonstrate our mastery of this machine, in the final week each student was required to go alone to some other class on campus, and there put on a film show. We were not told in advance what the class or the film would be. Mine turned out to be a class of student nurses, and their movie treat was a detailed depiction of a Caesarian birth delivery, in glorious technicolor.

Having led a rather sheltered life up to that point, I was both fascinated and horrified at what I suddenly found myself so unexpectedly witnessing on the screen. I remember beginning

to feel a little unwell . . . The next thing I knew, I was somehow lying face-up on the floor and staring at the ceiling. Someone had turned off the projector beside me and switched the lights back on, and a bevy of student nurses was crowded around me, eagerly loosening my clothing and fighting each other for a chance to administer first aid. How embarrassing! For the first time in my life, I had fainted!

But here is where the heroism comes in: I had a duty to perform! Staggering to my feet, and stoutly resisting all offers of further assistance, I commanded that the lights again be dimmed, and gallantly insisted on resuming my role as projectionist. The show went on! I'm proud to say that I did not faint again (at least, not until three years later, when giving—or rather, selling—some of my blood, to help finance a trip to Russia), and even managed to take occasional peeks at the screen. The great cause of Medicine had been served. I passed my course with an A (instead of possibly getting an F for Fainting), and went on to an inglorious, but mercifully brief, career in one of those gory mental operating theaters they call a High School Classroom.

The Malady Lingers On

Ironically, while my work and I have been becoming of increasing value to the Health Industry, that Establishment has been proving of very little value in helping me with my own health problems. I seem to specialize in suffering from conditions which are extremely bothersome and persistent, but in no way life-threatening or even seriously disabling, and are therefore of very little interest to any truly high-minded healer. Usually it costs a fancy price just to have the affliction given a fancy name. My current prize specimens are: Perennial Allergic Rhinitis (hay-fever), Circadian Disrhythmia (jet-lag), and Benign Muscular Fasciculations (twitches in the legs). In addition, I have an apparently above-average sensitivity to noise and tobacco smoke. (On the other hand, I seem to have a higher than average tolerance for radio and television news, extravagant praise, and funny mistakes made in print by other people.)

To Eat His Own

Sooner or later, however, I hope to overcome these various plagues, if only by outliving them—and Living Longer has therefore become one of my hobbies. In a truly logical and satisfactory world, the best way to ensure longevity would surely be always, and in every way, to pamper yourself. But in *this* world, for some regrettable reason, that doesn't seem to work. I myself, for example, am a certified food-lover of long-standing, but have lately allowed my own lifestyle to be much influenced by evidence that mice which are regularly made to fast live significantly longer than those always allowed to eat their fill. (For the purposes of this experiment, I am trying to forget that I am not a mouse.)

But even the healthiest of us have to eat now and then, and in recent years I have come to wonder if the word "Nutrition" begins with "Nut" because so many obviously nutty people seem to think they know something about it. My way of fighting back against the rising tide of nutritional reform and deprivation has so far been to meet it with such Brilliant Thoughts as: "WHEN ALL ELSE FAILS, EAT!" (no. 142); "BUT AFTER YOU HAVE GONE, I WILL STILL HAVE PEANUT-BUTTER" (no. 20); "ANYTHING IS GOOD, IF IT'S MADE OF CHOCOLATE" (no. 205); and "IS THERE A LIFE BEFORE BREAKFAST?" (no. 30). But these have been mere words on paper, and I have a grander form of revenge in mind. What I envision as my ultimate weapon in this Battle of the Aliments is a new form of foodstuff yet to be developed and put into production: the Edible Epigram. I see this as the culmination of a long, historic process, going on ever since symbolic value was first attached to certain foods and eating practices, and sanctified in one way or another by most religions, as in the sacrament of the Eucharist. One popular religious text indeed tells us that "In the beginning was the Word"—leading to the inevitable conclusion that the great "primordial soup," from which Science now speculates that all life sprang, was actually an Alphabet Soup.

Of course, we already have the printed cereal box, and

other forms of packaging, which enclose their edible contents with words, pictures, and messages of all kinds. And even further along in this thrilling continuum we find the Fortune Cookie, with the printed (but still, unfortunately, unassimilable) message actually enclosed by the food itself. Surely the time has now come for that final leap forward which will enable everybody to take in and absorb pieces of information through the mouth (until now only a one-way channel of communication), and thereby eliminate all remaining obstacles between the Reader's Digest and the reader's digestion.

I leave it to the gastronomical engineers to devise the specific substances and imprinting techniques which will make it possible for me, instead of mournfully eating my own words (as so often in the past), to have everybody else eating them, with gusto. In the meantime, however, words such as mine can serve only to console our psyches, while our stomachs continue to struggle with their unholy cravings, and we must fend off the nutritional and medicinal gnats, nits, and nuts as best as we can. As a great poet once said (in *Pot-Shot* no. 1291) "DON'T CRITICIZE MY EATING HABITS—I'VE GOT A CHOCOLATE CHIP ON MY SHOULDER."

I. Who Me

What am I to you? An image? A sequence of words? A disjointed cluster of ideas? No matter what meaning you see in me, it can never even approximate all that I mean to myself. After all, I take me wherever I go. My memories are full of me. My portrait waits for me in every mirror, my voice in every echo. When self-service is required, I am the only one who can help me.

What is to be done about this? If not satisfied with this self, to whom do I protest? Where are adjustments made, exchanges arranged, refunds given? How can I bear the responsibility of having this incredibly complex body and mind at my sole command? And what on earth am I to do about those many other sadly deluded bodies and minds I keep encountering, all of whom, without a single exception, insist on calling themselves "Me," and addressing me as "You"? If I knew the answers to any of these questions, I would probably never have had any of the following Brilliant Thoughts.

I WOULD NEVER
DELIBERATELY
HURT
MYSELF,

EXCEPT IN
SELF-DEFENCE.

© BRILLIANT ENTERPRISES 1972

Ashleigh
Brilliant

I WANT
TO BE TAKEN
SERIOUSLY~

ISN'T
THAT
A JOKE!

© ASHLEIGH BRILLIANT 1983.

POT-SHOTS NO. 2770.

BY WHAT
PROCESS
DID I
BECOME
A STRANGER
IN
MY OWN
LIFE?

Ashleigh Brilliant

POT-SHOTS NO. 342
Ashleigh Brilliant

I COME
FROM A GOOD HOME —

THAT'S WHY
THEY DON'T
WANT ME BACK.

Who Me 23

POT-SHOTS NO. 3119.

I'VE
ACCUMULATED
ENOUGH
TO BE THE ENVY
OF ALL
MY FRIENDS,

IF I HAD
ANY FRIENDS.

Ashleigh Brilliant

POT-SHOTS NO. 2581.

WATCH OUT!

IT'S
QUITE
POSSIBLE
THAT SOME
OF MY
BEST
MISTAKES
HAVEN'T YET
BEEN MADE.

POT-SHOTS NO. 2630.

WHY
DO I
KEEP
COMING
HOME,
EVERY TIME
I TRY
TO TRACE
MY TROUBLES
TO THEIR
SOURCE?

Ashleigh Brilliant

I'M A GOOD LEADER,

IF YOU DON'T TRY TO FOLLOW ME TOO CLOSELY.

Ashleigh Brilliant

The only reason why I have escaped capture is that nobody is interested in capturing me.

Ashleigh Brilliant

POT-SHOTS NO. 2430.

Ashleigh Brilliant

HOW CAN I BE SURE OF MY OWN ESSENTIAL WORTH,

WHEN THE EXCHANGE RATES CONTINUE TO FLUCTUATE?

POT-SHOTS NO. 2506.

I MAKE RULES FOR MYSELF QUITE EASILY,

BUT OFTEN HAVE GREAT DIFFICULTY IN ENFORCING THEM.

Ashleigh Brilliant

POT-SHOTS NO. 2455.

SOMETHING ABOUT ME MUST OBVIOUSLY GIVE LASTING SATISFACTION,

BECAUSE I'M VERY RARELY ASKED TO COME AGAIN.

Ashleigh Brilliant

I HAVE TO LIVE WITH MYSELF,

SO
I HAVE TO
TOLERATE
MANY
THINGS
I DISLIKE
ABOUT
ME.

POTENTIALLY,
I'M A
VERY DANGEROUS
INFLUENCE
ON
MYSELF,

BECAUSE
I KNOW
MY
WEAKNESSES
SO WELL.

© ASHLEIGH BRILLIANT 1982.

POT-SHOTS NO. 2647.

ALL PERSONS WHO APPEAR IN MY DREAMS SHOULD REALIZE THAT THEY DO SO AT THEIR OWN RISK.

Ashleigh Brilliant

© ASHLEIGH BRILLIANT 1983.

POT-SHOTS NO. 3154.

Somehow, I have to play my role in life as a gifted, beautiful, happy, well-adjusted person.

Ashleigh Brilliant

© ASHLEIGH BRILLIANT 1983.

POT-SHOTS NO. 3036.

Ashleigh Brilliant

I NEED AT LEAST ONE PERSON WHO BELIEVES IN ME, BUT SO FAR CAN'T EVEN RECRUIT MYSELF.

POT-SHOTS NO. 2617.

I TOO AM A MEMBER OF THE HUMAN RACE,

(BUT ADMITTEDLY NOT A VERY ACTIVE MEMBER).

© ASHLEIGH BRILLIANT 1982.

Ashleigh Brilliant

I CAN NO LONGER AFFORD MY UPKEEP,

POT-SHOTS NO. 1966.

BUT CAN'T FIND ANYBODY TO TAKE ME OFF MY HANDS.

© ASHLEIGH BRILLIANT 1980.

Ashleigh Brilliant

POT-SHOTS NO. 2695.

IT'S GOOD TO KNOW THAT, EVEN IF NOBODY ELSE NEEDS ME, I STILL DO.

© ASHLEIGH BRILLIANT 1983.

I WOULD
LIKE TO SPEAK
TO WHOEVER
IS IN CONTROL
OF MY LIFE,

AND SUGGEST
SOME
IMPROVEMENTS.

©ASHLEIGH BRILLIANT 1983.

©ASHLEIGH BRILLIANT 1983.

POT-SHOTS NO. 3084.

IT'S HARD ENOUGH
TO GET ALONG WITH
MY OWN FAMILY —
LET ALONE THE FAMILY OF MAN.

I'VE BEEN TRYING DESPERATELY TO SAVE MY MARRIAGE FOR THE LAST 35 YEARS.

Ashleigh Brilliant

NOW THAT I'VE MADE MY APPEARANCE,

CAN I MAKE MY DISAPPEARANCE?

Ashleigh Brilliant

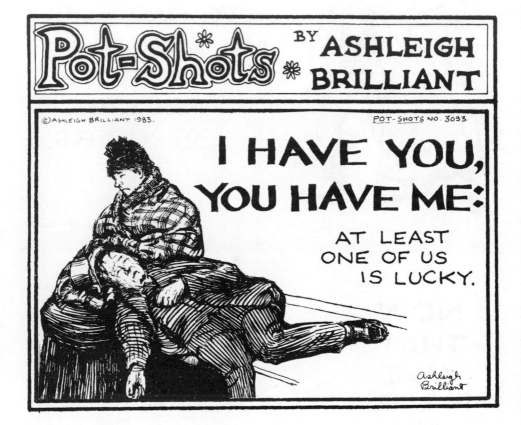

II. Are You There?

Nobody has ever clearly explained to me how a world like this, which, from all available evidence, exists only in my head (for example, it vanishes entirely whenever I close my eyes) ever came to be populated by a whole race of strange beings called Other People, many of whom I would never willingly have created. Making the best of an essentially impossible situation, I try to turn some of my close encounters with these unconsciously concocted creatures into elaborate games, with names like "Relationship" and "Communicate." Messages go back and forth between us—statements, requests, complaints, reassurances—as if there were any sense in getting involved with figments of one's own erratic imagination. I'm sorry to tell you that you are one of these figments, and, whatever your other attainments, you can never win the game of Being Me. As a consolation prize, however, I herewith present to you a group of Brilliant Thoughts which you may at least find useful in dealing with your fellow figments.

YOU MAY BE THE ANSWER TO MY PRAYERS,

BUT YOU'RE NOT THE ANSWER I WAS HOPING FOR.

Ashleigh Brilliant

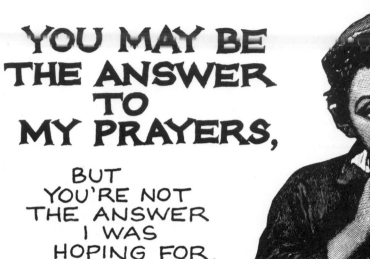

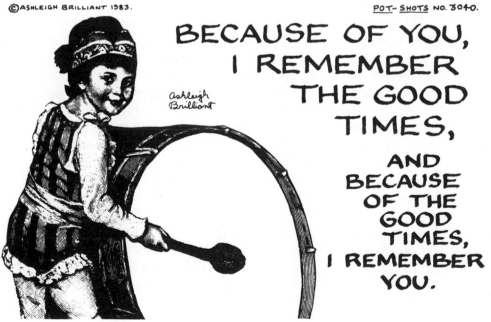

BECAUSE OF YOU, I REMEMBER THE GOOD TIMES,

AND BECAUSE OF THE GOOD TIMES, I REMEMBER YOU.

Ashleigh Brilliant

Ashleigh Brilliant

WHAT HAPPENED TO YOU COULD HAVE BEEN WORSE—

IT COULD HAVE HAPPENED TO ME.

LET'S MAKE IT DEFINITE:

I'LL SEE YOU WHEN I SEE YOU.

Ashleigh Brilliant

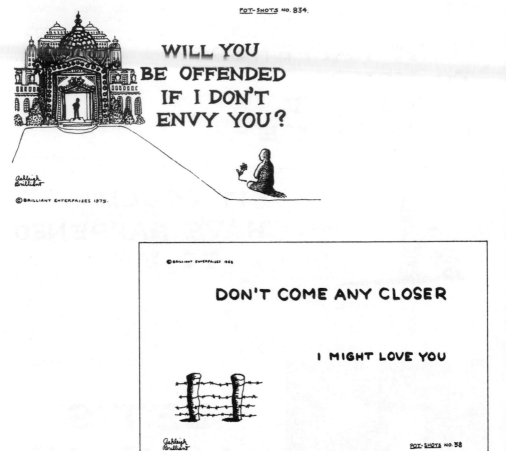

WILL YOU
BE OFFENDED
IF I DON'T
ENVY YOU?

© BRILLIANT ENTERPRISES 1975.

© BRILLIANT ENTERPRISES 1968

DON'T COME ANY CLOSER

I MIGHT LOVE YOU

POT-SHOTS NO. 58

© BRILLIANT ENTERPRISES 1969

POT-SHOTS NO. 140

HOW DARE YOU
GET ALONG
WITHOUT ME!

IS IT I
WHO AM FAR AWAY,
OR IS IT YOU?

I'M SO GLAD
I HAVE YOU
TO
ESCAPE
FROM.

Are You There? 37

HOW MUCH
DOES IT COST
TO BE
YOUR FRIEND?

Ashleigh
Brilliant

POT-SHOTS NO. 3027

WHAT GOOD
IS
YOUR LOVE,
IF
I CAN
NEVER
TAKE IT
FOR
GRANTED?

Ashleigh
Brilliant

POT-SHOTS NO. 792.

Ashleigh
Brilliant

WE MUST HAVE

COURAGE, FAITH,

AND

LUNCH TOGETHER

SOMETIME SOON.

WHAT MAKES ME WORTH SO MUCH TO ME, AND SO LITTLE TO YOU?

Ashleigh Brilliant

Can it be that I am destined for you, but you are not destined for me?

Ashleigh Brilliant

IF I DID ANYTHING WRONG, I'M SORRY —

IF I DID ANYTHING RIGHT, I'M PLEASANTLY SURPRISED.

YOU OBVIOUSLY NEED A PUSH ~

BUT HOW CAN I PUSH YOU TOWARDS ME?

BUT IF I YIELD TO YOUR REASONABLE DEMANDS,

I'LL NEVER
BE SAFE
FROM YOUR
REASONABLE
DEMANDS
AGAIN.

Ashleigh
Brilliant

Ashleigh
Brilliant

THINK OF ME
AS SOMEONE WHO
IS VERY OFTEN
THINKING
OF YOU.

Ashleigh
Brilliant

THE MORE
OFTEN
WE GET
TOGETHER,

THE LESS
SHOCKED
WE'LL BE
TO SEE
HOW MUCH
WE'VE
CHANGED.

Are You There? 41

POT-SHOTS NO. 3112.

YOU MAY NEVER LEARN TO UNDERSTAND ME ~

BUT,
IN TRYING,
YOU MAY
LEARN
TO LOVE ME.

Ashleigh Brilliant

POT-SHOTS NO. 3037.

CORRECT ME IF I'M WRONG,

AT
YOUR OWN
RISK.

Ashleigh Brilliant

POT-SHOTS NO. 2946.
Ashleigh Brilliant

Shall we consider
our relationship
satisfactory,
attempt to improve it,
or
abandon it
in despair?

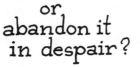

POT-SHOTS NO. 3059.

Ashleigh Brilliant

WE MIGHT BE BETTER OFF WITHOUT EACH OTHER ~

BUT IS THE EXPERIMENT WORTH THE RISK?

© ASHLEIGH BRILLIANT 1983

© ASHLEIGH BRILLIANT 1983.

POT-SHOTS NO. 2987.

AFTER ALL THESE YEARS,

HOW IS IT WE ARE STILL FRIENDS?

Ashleigh Brilliant

Are You There? 43

III. Confidence Tricks

Some matters are too private to be discussed in any way other than on postcards. As evidenced by this section, I have long been laboring to fill the need for truly intimate open communication. For a person like me, the task is not difficult, because I have always been willing to confide in the Universe at the slightest provocation. How else could I have written *Pot-Shot* no. 323: "I DON'T CARE WHAT THE WORLD KNOWS ABOUT ME—BUT I HOPE MY MOTHER NEVER FINDS OUT"?

Expressing your deeper feelings, without actually killing anybody, is widely recommended as a marvellous means of sweetening the mind, and clearing the channels that link it to other minds; and, according to many reports, people have been using my messages in quite serious (and sometimes even successful) efforts to heal sick friendships, save marriages, influence legislators,—even to forestall creditors (no. 707: HOW MUCH DO I OWE YOU, AND HOW LONG CAN I AVOID PAYING IT?")

Indeed, what begins to amaze me, after so many years of proclaiming so wondrous a gospel, is that there is still any war, crime, or other distress left in the world at all. Surely it can only be because, in a few key instances, the right *Pot-Shot* message has not yet reached the right recipient.

TODAY I HATE YOU

BUT TRY
ME AGAIN
TOMORROW.

Ashleigh
Brilliant

Ashleigh
Brilliant

IS IT
AN INVITATION
OR
A REJECTION
THAT
YOU HAVEN'T
THE COURAGE
TO GIVE ME?

YOU KNOW
I'LL ALWAYS HELP YOU
IF YOU NEED ME

SO PLEASE,
DON'T NEED ME.

Ashleigh Brilliant

Ashleigh Brilliant

HOW CAN
I HOPE
TO BE
SURE
ABOUT
YOU,

WHEN
I'M NOT
EVEN
SURE
ABOUT
ME?

POT-SHOTS NO. 3010.

WHY
DOESN'T IT
HURT YOU
MORE,
WHEN YOU
HURT
ME?

POT-SHOTS NO. 3104.

I KNOW
THERE IS
SOMETHING
TROUBLING
YOU ~

IS IT ME?

POT-SHOTS NO. 3122.

IT'S NOT THAT
I DON'T TRUST YOU

— OR
IS IT?

48

© ASHLEIGH BRILLIANT 1982.

APPARENTLY,
MY ROLE
IN LIFE
IS TO MAKE
YOU LAUGH,

WHILE YOURS
IS TO
MAKE ME
CRY.

Ashleigh Brilliant

POT-SHOTS NO. 2397.

Ashleigh Brilliant

MUST IT
ALWAYS BE
YOU AND ME
AGAINST
ME?

© ASHLEIGH BRILLIANT 1982.

© ASHLEIGH BRILLIANT 1983.

Ashleigh Brilliant

IT'S NOT
YOU
I'M
ANGRY
AT ~

I'M ANGRY
AT MYSELF,
FOR
LETTING YOU
UPSET ME.

Confidence Tricks 49

POT-SHOTS NO. 3116.

WHEN I CATCH YOU,

YOU'LL BE SORRY
THAT
YOU DIDN'T
LET ME
CATCH YOU
SOONER.

POT-SHOTS NO. 509

I'M VERY SENSITIVE TO PLEASURE —

PLEASE DON'T
COME TOO
NEAR ME.

HOW CAN I TRUST YOU,

IF I DON'T TRUST ALL THE PEOPLE YOU TRUST?

Ashleigh Brilliant

Ashleigh Brilliant

TO WHAT DO YOU ATTRIBUTE YOUR TOTAL LACK OF APPEAL?

I BLAME MYSELF FOR NOT

BLAMING YOU SOONER

Ashleigh Brilliant

ALLOW ME
TO CONGRATULATE YOU
ON THE SKILL
WITH WHICH
YOU HIDE
YOUR
DEFECTS.

SUDDENLY
I LOST
ALL CONTROL
OF MYSELF,

AND STARTED
MISSING
YOU.

POT-SHOTS NO. 1584.

©ASHLEIGH BRILLIANT 1980.

©BRILLIANT ENTERPRISES 1976

POT-SHOTS NO. 488

YOU MEET
ALL MY
REQUIREMENTS
FOR
TOTAL
REJECTION.

©BRILLIANT ENTERPRISES 1975.

POT-SHOTS NO. 880.

YOUR SNORING
DESERVES
A WIDER
AUDIENCE:

HAVE YOU
THOUGHT OF
PERFORMING
IN PUBLIC?

Confidence Tricks 53

HOW CAN I BE SURE

THAT
YOU
WANT ME
TO
BOTHER
YOU?

Ashleigh Brilliant

YOU KNOW I'D NEVER LEAVE YOU,

BUT PLEASE
DON'T PUT ME
IN A POSITION
WHERE I CAN'T.

Ashleigh Brilliant

PLEASE DON'T
JUSTIFY
MY
LACK OF
FAITH
IN YOU.

Ashleigh Brilliant

POT-SHOTS NO. 2413.

YESTERDAY,
    UPON MY BACK,
YOUR BURDEN
    SUDDENLY
        APPEARED ~

HOW DID
YOU DO IT?

Ashleigh Brilliant

WAIT! COME BACK!
THERE'S A PART OF MY FACE
YOU HAVEN'T STEPPED ON YET!

Ashleigh Brilliant

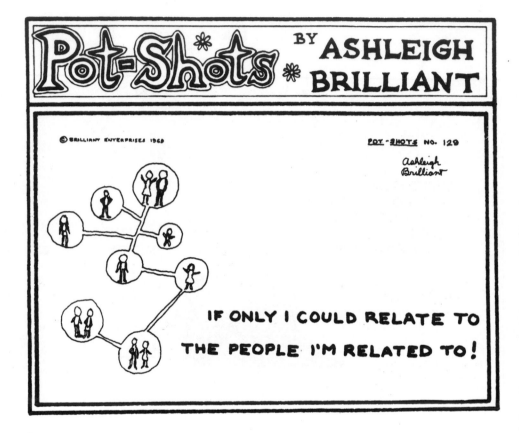

IV. Sense of Human

You can't always tell about People by looking at them, or listening to them, or even by being married to them. No matter how attractively packaged they may come, and regardless of all guarantees, various peculiarities will inevitably emerge to surprise, perplex, and frustrate whoever has to deal with them. Just why People are so odd is still a matter of scientific conjecture. Some believe it can be accounted for by the "Big Bang" theory, whereby everything in the Universe (including People) is supposedly becoming more distant from everything else, and therefore presumably harder for everything else (or everybody else) to understand. This, however, would fail to explain how it happens that we so often, and in so many different ways, collide with one another.

I myself have for many years been seeking a safe structure from which to observe and report upon this continuing war between sanity and humanity. So far, I've discovered no more secure vantage-point than one which combines the architectural features of an Ivory Tower with those of a House of Cards. Perhaps some of the following cards may provide suitable material for strengthening your own fortifications.

POT-SHOTS NO. 2482.

NEVER EXPECT FAIRNESS,

WHERE MY VITAL INTERESTS ARE CONCERNED.

Ashleigh Brilliant

POT-SHOTS NO. 2537.

LIFE CAN BE VERY DEEP,

BUT I'M TRYING TO STAY AT THE SHALLOW END.

Ashleigh Brilliant

POT-SHOTS NO. 2588.

LORD, HELP ME TO MEET THIS SELF-IMPOSED AND TOTALLY UNNECESSARY CHALLENGE.

Ashleigh
Brilliant

POT-SHOTS NO. 2798.

Ashleigh
Brilliant

SOMETHING IN ME STILL FEELS THE SAME WAY I DID BEFORE I CHANGED MY MIND.

POT-SHOTS NO. 2555.

WAKE ME UP

WHEN
EVERYTHING
IS
ORGANIZED.

Ashleigh Brilliant

 POT-SHOTS NO. 2411.

GET OUT OF MY WAY! —
I'M IN A HURRY
TO GO HOME AND RELAX.

Ashleigh Brilliant

 POT-SHOTS NO. 2520.

ONE OF THE FUNNIEST
THINGS ABOUT
PEOPLE
IS
HOW THEY
DIFFER
IN WHAT
THEY
THINK IS
FUNNY.

Ashleigh Brilliant

POT-SHOTS NO. 380

HOW CAN YOU
CALL IT
UNREASONABLE

WHEN ALL
I WANT
IS MY
OWN WAY?

©BRILLIANT ENTERPRISES 1972

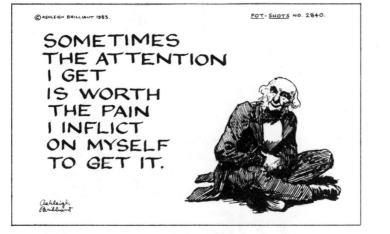

©ASHLEIGH BRILLIANT 1983.   POT-SHOTS NO. 2840.

SOMETIMES
THE ATTENTION
I GET
IS WORTH
THE PAIN
I INFLICT
ON MYSELF
TO GET IT.

©ASHLEIGH BRILLIANT 1983.   POT-SHOTS NO. 3064.

SOME THINGS
LEAVE MY LIST
AFTER I'VE DONE THEM ~

OTHERS
AFTER
I'VE
ABANDONED
HOPE
OF
DOING
THEM.

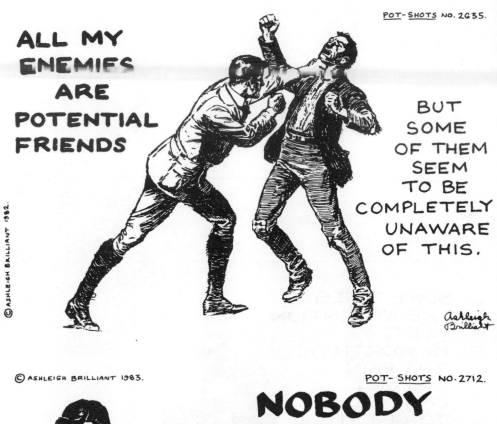

ALL MY
ENEMIES
ARE
POTENTIAL
FRIENDS

BUT
SOME
OF THEM
SEEM
TO BE
COMPLETELY
UNAWARE
OF THIS.

Ashleigh
Brilliant

NOBODY
CAN CHANGE
THE ENTIRE
WORLD,

BUT
EVERY WOMAN
CAN
AT LEAST TRY
TO CHANGE
SOME MAN.

Ashleigh
Brilliant

I'D. LIKE TO SHOW YOU WHO'S BOSS,

BUT AM AFRAID IT WOULD ONLY CONFIRM THAT YOU ARE.

Ashleigh Brilliant

I KNOW I NEED TO LEARN PATIENCE:

WHERE CAN I TAKE A CRASH COURSE?

Ashleigh Brilliant

I WANT TO DOMINATE ~

TO WHOM SHOULD I APPLY FOR PERMISSION?

Ashleigh Brilliant

HOW CAN SO MANY THINGS I'VE NO MORE USE FOR STILL HAVE SO MUCH MEANING FOR ME?

POT-SHOTS NO. 2829. ©ASHLEIGH BRILLIANT 1983.

A GOOD
FRIEND
IS WORTH
PURSUING ~

BUT WHY
WOULD
A GOOD FRIEND
BE
RUNNING AWAY?

Ashleigh
Brilliant

POT-SHOTS NO. 2673.

A FATE
WORSE THAN DEATH:

TO BE
MARRIED
ALIVE.

©ASHLEIGH BRILLIANT 1982.

Ashleigh Brilliant

©ASHLEIGH BRILLIANT 1982.

POT-SHOTS
NO. 2668.

NEXT
TIME,

I INTEND
TO BE
THOROUGHLY
PREPARED

Ashleigh
Brilliant

FOR LAST TIME.

IT'S SOMETIMES
EASIER
TO INSIST ON
BEING WRONG
THAN IT IS
TO ADMIT
BEING IGNORANT.

Ashleigh Brilliant

MY LIFE
IS MY
RESPONSIBILITY,

BUT I CAN
ALWAYS USE
A LITTLE HELP.

Ashleigh Brilliant

IT'S ALWAYS
POSSIBLE
THAT
I'M WRONG ~

BUT
THAT'S NEVER
AT THE TOP
OF MY LIST
OF POSSIBILITIES.

Ashleigh Brilliant

SOMEWHERE
THERE
OUGHT
TO BE
A CLUB

FOR
ANTI-SOCIAL
PEOPLE.

Ashleigh
Brilliant

POT - SHOTS NO. 523

Why should I
be willing to compromise,

When I'm the one
who's right?

Ashleigh
Brilliant

v. What's in a World?

In the unlikely event that you ever begin to lose interest in your own affairs, there are always plenty more, of even greater variety, in a place now reachable by many forms of transportation, known as the World. Here you will find any number of strange and compelling attractions, all the more fascinating because most of them, as far as any possible need for you has ever been concerned, are entirely self-sustaining. Without your advice or consent, whole cities have been built, libraries of books written, entire cultures and civilizations organized, and an enormously complicated system called Nature set up. Almost anywhere you go in this great bewilderness, it will not be hard to find places you don't know, people you have never heard of, and things you don't understand.

None of this, however, should discourage you from embarking on any well-equipped voyage of discovery, since there would otherwise hardly be anything for you to discover. But be sure to take along a good supply of trading-trinkets, such as these *Brilliant Thoughts,* which are still utterly unknown in some benighted localities, and worth their weight in friendly smiles.

I'M DEFINITELY IN FAVOR OF HUMAN SURVIVAL,

BUT NOT NECESSARILY AT ALL COSTS.

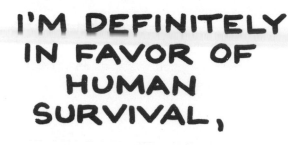

Ashleigh Brilliant

Ashleigh
Brilliant

I'VE TRIED TALKING TO ANIMALS,

BUT IT'S NO USE —

 their minds are usually already made up.

POT-SHOTS NO. 2701.

ONE THING TRAVEL TEACHES IS WHY LIVING AT HOME IS SO POPULAR.

Ashleigh Brilliant

POT-SHOTS NO. 3009.

Ashleigh Brilliant

THE MOST EFFECTIVE PROTECTION AGAINST THEFT

IS TO HAVE NOTHING WORTH STEALING.

I NEVER
MISS
REALITY
WHEN I'M
NOT
IN IT,

BUT IT'S SOMETIMES
NICE TO COME BACK TO.

Ashleigh
Brilliant

DON'T
EXPECT ME
TO STRAIGHTEN UP,
WHEN
IT'S ALL I CAN DO
TO KEEP FROM
FALLING OVER.

Ashleigh
Brilliant

IT'S REMARKABLE HOW MUCH
THE WEATHER AFFECTS MY LIFE,

AND
HOW
LITTLE
MY LIFE
AFFECTS
THE
WEATHER.

Ashleigh
Brilliant

There may be no Heaven anywhere,
But somewhere there is
A San Francisco.

Ashleigh Brilliant

POT-SHOTS
No. 168

POT-SHOTS NO. 2748.

MOST OF MY THREATS
DO ME
NO GOOD
AT ALL,

IF I
HAVE TO
CARRY THEM OUT.

Ashleigh
Brilliant

POT-SHOTS NO. 2795.

THERE OUGHT TO BE A BETTER WAY THAN GOVERNMENT TO RUN THE WORLD.

Ashleigh
Brilliant

POT-SHOTS NO. 3095.

Ashleigh
Brilliant

KEEP DOING OPENLY WHAT'S NOT SOCIALLY APPROVED, AND EVENTUALLY SOCIETY WILL CHANGE...

OR YOU'LL BE KILLED.

POT-SHOTS NO. 2706.

WHAT SHOULD I WEAR FOR THE NEXT DISASTER?

Ashleigh
Brilliant

To the Tax Office:
All is over between us.
Please don't attempt to
communicate
with me
again.

Ashleigh Brilliant

Ashleigh Brilliant

HOW CAN WE
HAVE A MUTINY

 IF NOBODY'S
IN COMMAND?

MODERN TRAVEL WOULD BE TOTALLY DELIGHTFUL, IF I COULD ONLY LEARN TO ENJOY BOREDOM, DISCOMFORT, AND FATIGUE.

READY ~ AIM ~ SPEND!

EVERY NEIGHBORHOOD SEEMS TO CONTAIN A FEW DIFFICULT PEOPLE, AND ONE OR TWO WHO ARE ABSOLUTELY IMPOSSIBLE.

POT-SHOTS NO. 2714.

PRESERVE THE PEOPLE'S RIGHT TO THE LAND,

AND THE LAND'S RIGHT TO BE PROTECTED FROM THE PEOPLE.

Ashleigh Brilliant

POT-SHOTS NO. 2843.

WHY IS
NOISE
SO OFTEN
SO MUCH
MORE ENJOYABLE
TO MAKE
THAN
TO BE
FORCED TO HEAR?

Ashleigh Brilliant

POT-SHOTS NO. 2711.

Ashleigh Brilliant

THE
REAL
PENALTY
FOR
LITTERING
IS HAVING
TO LIVE
IN A
DIRTY
COUNTRY.

What's in a World? 77

POT-SHOTS NO. 2547.

THE TRUE ARTIST

IS ONE WHO
INSISTS ON
PRODUCING
A SUPPLY,
WHETHER
OR NOT
THERE'S
ANY DEMAND.

 POT-SHOTS NO. 2850.

MY LIFE
HAS BEEN
GREATLY
INFLUENCED
BY MANY BOOKS
WHICH I
HAVE NEVER READ.

 POT-SHOTS NO. 2720.

DON'T WORK TOO HARD ~

OR
IT MAY
REVEAL
THAT
THE REST
OF US
AREN'T WORKING
HARD ENOUGH.

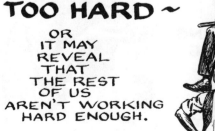

POT-SHOTS NO. 2920.

NO JOURNEY IS EVER COMPLETE UNTIL YOU COME HOME AGAIN,

OR UNTIL SOME NEW PLACE BECOMES HOME.

Ashleigh Brilliant

 POT-SHOTS NO. 3158.

HISTORY MAY NEVER HAVE ALL THE FACTS,

BUT HISTORY ALWAYS HAS THE LAST WORD.

Ashleigh Brilliant

VI. Say La Vie

Most of us who are alive consider it essential to remain in that condition as long as we can, even though it is notoriously beset with dangers and difficulties. One way of trying to get through them, and to help others in the same predicament who might otherwise lose heart, is to mark the way with meaningful inscriptions. This practice has a long and honorable history, going back to the cave paintings with which our primitive ancestors advertised their primitive concerns and problems. Today, in keeping with our state-of-the-art neuroses, we have more sophisticated forms of publication, including one for which I am happy to take whatever credit you want to give— the *Pot Shot* Postcard, which might be thought of as a sort of cave painting on the roof of the brain.

Deceptively innocent at first glance, with their varied colors and my artless art, these cards actually represent a very highly concentrated form of mental energy, and should never be allowed to fall into the wrong minds. The following section will demonstrate what wild sparks can be generated when this power of super-communication is brought to bear upon matter as daunting and delicate as the subject of Everyday Life.

THE CLOSER I GET TO MY GOAL,

THE BETTER
MY CHANCE
OF DISCOVERING
WHAT IT IS.

Ashleigh
Brilliant

IN ORDER
TO BE READY
WHEN NEEDED,

YOU MUST
(UNFORTUNATELY)
ALSO
BE READY
WHEN
NOT NEEDED.

Ashleigh Brilliant

FIRST
I LOST
MY
INNOCENCE;

NOW
I AM TRYING
TO LOSE
MY GUILT.

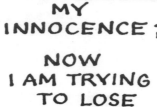

POT-SHOTS NO. 3087.

WHY DO
SO MANY OF
MY MISTAKES

REFUSE
TO
GO
AWAY?

POT-SHOTS NO. 2427.

IF I DO
ENOUGH
DIFFERENT
THINGS
IN ENOUGH
DIFFERENT
WAYS,

I MAY,
EVENTUALLY,
DO
SOMETHING
RIGHT.

KEEP PUNISHING YOURSELF
— YOU PROBABLY
DESERVE IT.

Ashleigh Brilliant

POT-SHOTS NO. 3050.

IT SEEMS UNFAIR ~

I DON'T ASK MUCH
OF LIFE,
YET LIFE
KEEPS ASKING
SO MUCH OF ME.

Ashleigh Brilliant

POT-SHOTS NO. 2813.

SUCCESS AHEAD
IS ALWAYS
BETTER
THAN
SUCCESS
BEHIND:

THE ONLY
DISADVANTAGE IS:
  IT'S SLIGHTLY
  LESS CERTAIN.

Ashleigh Brilliant

SOMETIMES
IT TAKES COURAGE
TO SAY NO,

OR TO SAY YES,

OR EVEN
TO SAY ANYTHING.

Ashleigh Brilliant

 Ashleigh Brilliant

WHY SHOULD I LET YOU
INTO MY PRIVATE HELL?

TRY TO AVOID
GOING THROUGH THE WORLD
TOO FAST,

OR IT
WILL
ALL
BECOME

A
BLUR.

Ashleigh Brilliant

POT-SHOTS NO. 2960.

SOMETIMES
MY MIND
IS SO
UNCOMFORTABLE,

I WISH
I COULD
GO SOMEWHERE
AND
TAKE IT OFF.

Ashleigh Brilliant

POT-SHOTS NO. 3002.

THE
SUREST
WAY TO
LEARN
IS BY
DOING IT ~

BUT OFTEN,
THE LESSON IS:
DON'T DO IT!

Ashleigh
Brilliant

POT-SHOTS NO. 2641.

Ashleigh
Brilliant

The
only thing
that keeps
me going
is that
I've forgotten
how to stop.

Ashleigh Brilliant

I'm worried about the possible existence of things that would worry me if I knew about them.

MY LIFE WOULD NOT MAKE A GOOD DRAMA —

THE CHARACTERS ARE NOT SUFFICIENTLY BELIEVABLE.

Ashleigh Brilliant

THE BEST
WAY TO
GET
THROUGH
A LONG,
DARK
NIGHT

IS BY
SLEEPING
THROUGH IT.

IN ORDER
FOR ME
TO DO BETTER
NEXT TIME,
ONE THING
IS ESSENTIAL:

TO
SURVIVE
THIS
TIME.

I WANT
A SIGNED
APOLOGY

FROM THE WORLD,
FOR THE WAY
IT HAS BEEN TREATING ME.

I WOULDN'T
MISS
WHAT I'VE LOST
SO MUCH,
IF I COULD
ONLY FORGET
I EVER
HAD IT.

Ashleigh Brilliant

MY CONDITION HAS
NO KNOWN CAUSE
AND NO
KNOWN CURE,

BUT
FORTUNATELY
ALSO
NO KNOWN
SYMPTOMS.

Ashleigh Brilliant

I DON'T
KNOW
WHAT I'M
LOOKING FOR~

THAT'S WHAT
MAKES
THE SEARCH
SO EXCITING!

Ashleigh Brilliant

MY LIFE SHOWS
A CLEAR PATTERN

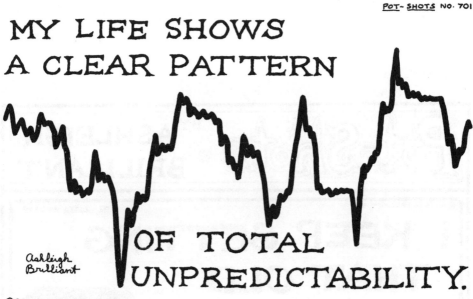

OF TOTAL
UNPREDICTABILITY.

Ashleigh
Brilliant

© BRILLIANT ENTERPRISES 1974.

© BRILLIANT ENTERPRISES 1971   POT-SHOTS NO. 259

I AM
EAGERLY AWAITING
MY NEXT
DISAPPOINTMENT.

Ashleigh Brilliant

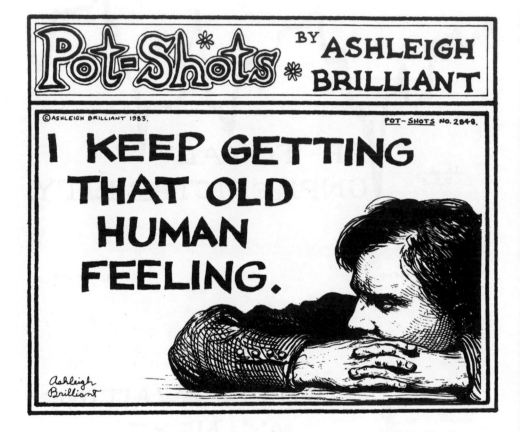

VII. Feelthy Thoughts

Regardless of the condition of our sensory organs, we all have what are known as Feelings. Even groups, even nations, sometimes claim to have them. This would not be a big problem if everybody had the same ones at the same time, or if we could at least know and understand those of everybody else. No such luck. As far as Feelings go, the world is a morass, in which a truly desperate person will clutch even at a postcard.

The following cards have somehow emerged from the ooze of my own emotional life, despite efforts to suppress them with liberal doses of vitamins and exercise. Feelings are persistent creatures, and are more than likely, if left too long unattended, to send up great howls of protest. It should be apparent, from this noisy collection, that you and I have something in common, although I admit it is not necessarily anything to give either of us much cause for celebration.

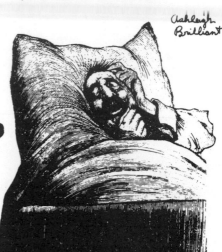

NOTHING IS WORSE THAN THE AGONY OF INDECISION,

EXCEPT THE GRIEF OF HAVING DECIDED WRONGLY.

Ashleigh Brilliant

WHY IS EVERYBODY BEHAVING AS IF THERE WERE NO REASON TO PANIC ?

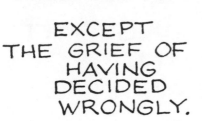

Ashleigh Brilliant

MY
GREAT
AMBITION
IS
TO SECURE
A
SPEAKING PART
IN
MY OWN LIFE.

Ashleigh Brilliant

ALL I WANT
IS A WARM BED
AND A KIND WORD
AND
UNLIMITED
POWER.

Ashleigh Brilliant

POT-SHOTS NO. 3055.

HOW DISTURBING!

NO MATTER
WHERE I AM
OR
WHAT I'M DOING,

I'M ALWAYS
MISSING
SOMETHING
SOMEWHERE
ELSE.

Ashleigh Brilliant

POT-SHOTS NO. 2824.

Ashleigh Brilliant

I'LL BE GLAD WHEN
ALL THE BAD PARTS
OF LIFE
ARE OVER,
AND
ONLY GOOD PARTS
REMAIN.

POT-SHOTS NO. 2696.

Ashleigh Brilliant

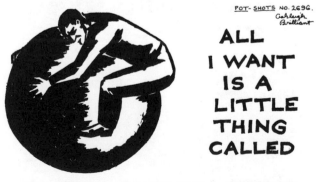

ALL
I WANT
IS A
LITTLE
THING
CALLED

TOTAL SATISFACTION.

96

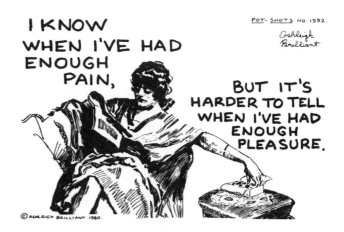

I KNOW WHEN I'VE HAD ENOUGH PAIN,

BUT IT'S HARDER TO TELL WHEN I'VE HAD ENOUGH PLEASURE.

POT-SHOTS NO. 1992.

Ashleigh Brilliant

©ASHLEIGH BRILLIANT 1980.

POT-SHOTS NO. 2730.

SOMETIMES THE WORST POSSIBLE PUNISHMENT IS TO BE COMPLETELY FORGIVEN.

Ashleigh Brilliant

©ASHLEIGH BRILLIANT 1983.

©ASHLEIGH BRILLIANT 1983.

POT-SHOTS NO. 3111.

Ashleigh Brilliant

HOW CAN YOU POSSIBLY CONSIDER YOUR OWN HAPPINESS MORE IMPORTANT THAN MINE?

Feelthy Thoughts 97

WHY HAVE I BEEN SINGLED OUT TO BE SO ORDINARY?

Ashleigh Brilliant

© ASHLEIGH BRILLIANT 1980

© ASHLEIGH BRILLIANT 1983.

ISN'T IT STRANGE
HOW MANY
OF OUR
SECRET
SENSITIVITIES
ARE
THE SAME
AS THOSE
OF
EVERYBODY
ELSE.

Ashleigh Brilliant

I AM TORN BY CONFLICTING APATHIES.

© ASHLEIGH BRILLIANT 1983.

Ashleigh Brilliant

I HOPE YOU'RE FEELING.

Ashleigh Brilliant

Ashleigh Brilliant

I'M THINKING
OF QUITTING
ALL MY
ACTIVITIES,

IN ORDER TO DEVOTE FULL-TIME TO MY BOREDOM.

NOT EVERYTHING I DISLIKE SHOULD BE DESTROYED:

SOME OF IT
SHOULD SIMPLY BE
MOVED FARTHER AWAY.

Ashleigh Brilliant

ISN'T ANYBODY INTERESTED IN EXPLOITING MY FATAL WEAKNESS FOR PLEASURE?

Ashleigh Brilliant

NOT NOW

AND MAYBE
NOT LATER EITHER.

Ashleigh Brilliant

I MAY BE FORGOTTEN

BUT I'M
NOT GONE

Ashleigh Brilliant

POT-SHOTS NO. 2977.

I WISH
I COULD FEEL
MORE NEEDED,

WITHOUT
FEELING OBLIGED
TO FILL
THE NEED.

POT-SHOTS NO. 2835.

NEVER FALL IN LOVE
WITH
ANYBODY
YOU CAN'T
AFFORD TO LOSE.

THEY LAUGHED AT EDISON AND EINSTEIN,

BUT SOMEHOW I STILL FEEL UNCOMFORTABLE WHEN THEY LAUGH AT ME.

Ashleigh Brilliant

Ashleigh Brilliant

IF I CAN'T GET WHAT I WANT FROM YOU,

I'LL GO AWAY,

AND GET IT FROM NOBODY.

BOOKS HAVE MADE ME LAUGH AND CRY,

BUT, UNFORTUNATELY, NO BOOK HAS EVER LOVED ME.

Ashleigh Brilliant

I AM HOPING
VERY SOON
TO HAVE
SOMETHING
TO HOPE FOR.

Ashleigh Brilliant

BEFORE WE MAKE LOVE,
WOULD YOU MIND TAKING OUT THE GARBAGE?

Ashleigh Brilliant

IF I DON'T
DO IT TODAY,

WHAT
WILL I HAVE
TO BE GLAD
OR SORRY ABOUT
TOMORROW?

Ashleigh Brilliant

I KNOW WHICH WAY
THE WIND IS BLOWING...
BUT I STILL
     HAVE TO FOLLOW
MY OWN COURSE.

Ashleigh Brilliant

POT-SHOTS NO. 177

POT-SHOTS NO. 2493.

SOMETIMES
I WISH
I COULD GIVE
ALL MY
EMOTIONS

THE DAY
OFF.

Ashleigh
Brilliant

Pot-Shots

BY ASHLEIGH BRILLIANT

© BRILLIANT ENTERPRISES 1971

POT-SHOTS NO. 292

The Mind is a Wonderful Thing —

EVERYBODY SHOULD HAVE ONE!

Ashleigh Brilliant

VIII. Mind If I Think

Thinking is a very refined form of Feeling, in which the brain serves as a highly specialized set of fingertips, attempting to feel their way through the murky maze we call the Cosmos. People have probably been doing it for thousands of years, but, despite its great antiquity, Thinking has never achieved the prestige accorded to many other activities of lesser lineage. It has, for example, no status as an athletic event. No prizes are offered for the Year's Best Thought. As far as popularity is concerned, great thinkers of either sex are less likely to be in demand than great drinkers.

Nevertheless, some of us persist, almost in spite of ourselves. The thoughts presented here are of course only a small part of the thinking I have done in my life. Some of my best thinking was done before I learned to speak, and has unfortunately been lost. Some was considered in excessively good taste, and has therefore been suppressed. What remains, I should caution you, is not intended to be taken in large doses, or it may bring on a torpid condition known as Too Much. Chronic sufferers from this disorder should probably think about joining Over-Thinkers Anonymous—No, wait,—on second thought, they should probably not think about anything at all.

POT-SHOTS NO. 2836.

SOMETIMES
I MAKE
A MENTAL
NOTE,
BUT THEN
FORGET
WHERE
I PUT IT.

Ashleigh Brilliant

POT-SHOTS NO. 2831.

IT WOULD SAVE
SO MUCH TIME,
IF WE COULD
ALL BE BORN
KNOWING
EVERYTHING
THAT'S
ALREADY
KNOWN.

Ashleigh Brilliant

POT-SHOTS NO. 3021.

I AM IN FAVOR OF SELF-RELIANCE,

ESPECIALLY IF IT PREVENTS OTHER PEOPLE FROM RELYING ON ME.

Ashleigh Brilliant

POT-SHOTS NO. 2880.

IT'S TRUE I'M A SLOW LEARNER,

BUT I COMPENSATE BY BEING A FAST FORGETTER.

Ashleigh Brilliant

POT-SHOTS NO. 2752.

NEW SHORTAGE:

NO TIME GOES ON,

FEWER AND FEWER THINGS HAVE NEVER BEEN DONE BEFORE.

Ashleigh Brilliant

POT-SHOTS NO. 2838.
Ashleigh Brilliant

Beware! the very words you're now reading were possibly written by an infinite number of monkeys.

POT-SHOTS No. 2741.

EVERYTHING TAKES LONGER THAN YOU EXPECT ~

EVEN WHEN YOU EXPECT IT TO TAKE LONGER THAN YOU EXPECT.

Ashleigh Brilliant

SUCCESS, FOR SOME PEOPLE, DEPENDS ON BECOMING WELL-KNOWN;

POT-SHOTS NO. 2437.

Ashleigh Brilliant

FOR OTHERS, IT DEPENDS ON NEVER BEING FOUND OUT.

POT-SHOTS NO. 2372.

WHY SHOULD READERS BE ABLE TO READ SO FAST WHAT IT TOOK WRITERS SO LONG TO WRITE?

Ashleigh Brilliant

Mind If I Think   111

Ashleigh Brilliant POT-SHOTS No. 516

ISN'T IT A WONDERFUL SYSTEM WHEN EVERYBODY HAS A BIRTHDAY IN THE SAME YEAR!

 POT-SHOTS NO. 2451.

I STUDIED GEOMETRY, BUT NEVER FOUND OUT WHETHER LIFE IS A STRAIGHT LINE OR A CIRCLE.

Ashleigh Brilliant

 POT-SHOTS NO. 2490.

THE SAME PIECE OF TROUBLE CAN BE BIG OR SMALL, DEPENDING ENTIRELY ON WHOSE IT IS.

Ashleigh Brilliant

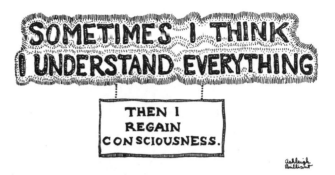

SOMETIMES I THINK
I UNDERSTAND EVERYTHING

THEN I
REGAIN
CONSCIOUSNESS.

Ashleigh
Brilliant

PURELY BY CHANCE,
THE IDEA
CAME TO ME
THAT NOTHING
EVER HAPPENS
PURELY BY CHANCE.

Ashleigh Brilliant

UNFORTUNATELY,
IT'S POSSIBLE
TO BE ABLE
TO DO SOMETHING
EXTREMELY WELL

Ashleigh
Brilliant

THAT
NOBODY
EVER
WANTS
DONE.

POT-SHOTS NO. 3053.

DOING IT WRONG FAST

IS
AT LEAST
BETTER
THAN
DOING IT
WRONG
SLOWLY.

Ashleigh Brilliant

POT-SHOTS NO. 2882.

Ashleigh Brilliant

CHANGE ENOUGH OF THE LITTLE PICTURES,

AND
YOU'LL FIND
YOU'VE CHANGED
THE BIG PICTURE.

114

I LOVE
INFORMATION ~

WHAT I DON'T LIKE
IS HAVING TO
DO SOMETHING WITH IT.

Ashleigh Brilliant

WHICH CAME FIRST:

THE
GOOD TIMES
OR THE
BAD TIMES?

Ashleigh Brilliant

THIS
IS
NO
TIME
TO BE
REASONABLE!

Ashleigh Brilliant

Mind If I Think 115

THINKING IS GOOD EXERCISE FOR THE BRAIN ~

BUT
UNFORTUNATELY
THIS APPLIES
TO BOTH RIGHT AND
WRONG THINKING.

Ashleigh Brilliant

IF IT CAN'T
BE DONE IN BED,

IT'S PROBABLY
NOT
WORTH
DOING.

Ashleigh Brilliant

ONE WAY
TO MAKE A
BIG MISTAKE
IS
TO START BY
PUTTING
MANY
SMALL
MISTAKES
TOGETHER.

Ashleigh Brilliant

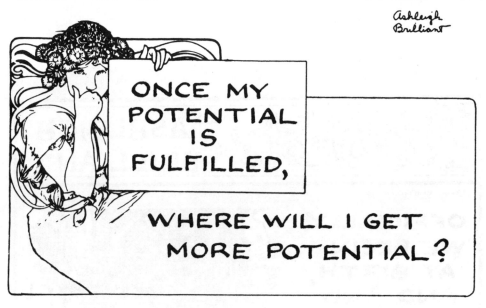

POT-SHOTS NO. 2507.

ONCE MY
POTENTIAL
IS
FULFILLED,

WHERE WILL I GET
MORE POTENTIAL?

POT-SHOTS NO. 2626.

REASONABLE
THOUGHT
CAN ONLY GO
SO FAR...

BEYOND THAT,
YOU MUST
EITHER
BE UNREASONABLE
OR
STOP THINKING.

Pot-Shots BY ASHLEIGH BRILLIANT

POT-SHOTS NO. 2782.

OFFICIALLY,
WE BEGIN
AT BIRTH,
AND END
AT DEATH,

BUT
IT'S REALLY
MUCH MORE
COMPLICATED
THAN THAT.

Ashleigh Brilliant

IX. All Change

Some time ago, I began to notice that things do not always stay the same. Considerable research led to the conclusion that this is the fault of a mischievious and rather mysterious entity called Change, some of whose antics are investigated in the following pages.

If we must have them at all, I personally would prefer all changes to be for the better; but this is not always easy to arrange on notice as short as a single lifetime. One could, I suppose, at least insist that only necessary changes be permitted, but that would only provoke endless arguments about such questions as whether this entire Century has been at all necessary.

Perhaps a more pragmatic approach might be to try to change yourself at the same rate that everything else is changing. This can, however, be somewhat exhausting, and may very well account for the large numbers of people who were alive in 1653, but no longer are today.

In the final analysis, it appears that we can blame all change on the phenomenon known as Time. So, if we don't like the changes we see happening, all we need to do is arrange to have Time abolished, or at least permanently "frozen" at some internationally agreed-upon moment. Should that ever come to pass, I naturally hope that the moment selected will, if possible, be one when it's a nice day everywhere.

WHAT IF NOTHING EVER HAPPENS TO ME?

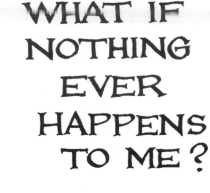

Ashleigh Brilliant

POT-SHOTS NO. 3072.

A HUNDRED MILLION YEARS FROM NOW, I MAY HAVE BEEN FORGOTTEN BY ALL BUT A FEW.

Ashleigh Brilliant

NOTHING CAN WEAR YOU DOWN MORE COMPLETELY THAN LIFE.

Ashleigh
Brilliant

WHEN DEATH IS EVENTUALLY ABOLISHED,

HOW WILL PEOPLE EVER UNDERSTAND WHAT IT WAS LIKE TO BE MORTAL?

Ashleigh
Brilliant

IF ONLY
THERE
WERE
SOME WAY
TO LEARN
IN ADVANCE

WHOSE
SIDE
TIME
IS ON.

Ashleigh Brilliant

Is it better
to die
before
your memories,

or
to have
your
memories
die first?

Ashleigh Brilliant

POT-SHOTS NO. 2531.

IF I'VE COME
THIS FAR
ALREADY,

THINK HOW FAR
I CAN GO
IF
I NEVER
DIE.

Ashleigh
Brilliant

POT-SHOTS NO. 2797.

IT'S TRUE
I'M GETTING
OLDER,

BUT THERE ARE STILL
MANY GOOD HUGS
LEFT IN ME.

Ashleigh
Brilliant

POT-SHOTS NO. 2927.

PEOPLE WHO
NEED TO
GET OLDER

ARE
MUCH
LUCKIER
THAN
PEOPLE WHO
NEED TO
GET YOUNGER.

Ashleigh
Brilliant

All Change 123

POT-SHOTS NO. 2753.

MORE TIME BEHIND ME MEANS LESS TIME AHEAD ~

BUT AT LEAST THE TOTAL IS ALWAYS THE SAME.

Ashleigh Brilliant

POT-SHOTS NO. 2735.   © ASHLEIGH BRILLIANT 1983.

I MUSTN'T DIE YET! I STILL HAVE SO MUCH THINKING TO DO!

Ashleigh Brilliant

POT-SHOTS NO. 2447.

ONE THING HASN'T CHANGED:

THE PEOPLE WHO WERE MY AGE YEARS AGO ARE STILL MY AGE TODAY.

Ashleigh Brilliant

POT-SHOTS NO. 2747.

Children
who are
born into
happy
families
grow up
speaking love
as their
native language.

©ASHLEIGH BRILLIANT 1983.

©ASHLEIGH BRILLIANT 1983. POT-SHOTS NO. 2772.

I DON'T THINK I CAN FACE ANOTHER YEAR OF ANNUAL EVENTS.

©ASHLEIGH BRILLIANT 1983. POT-SHOTS NO. 3052.

CONSIDERING
THE DIRECTION
THINGS ARE GOING,

IT'S IMPOSSIBLE
TO PREDICT
IN WHICH
DIRECTION
THEY'LL
BE
GOING
NEXT.

I MIGHT NEVER
HAVE LEFT
THE GOOD TIMES,
IF I'D
REALIZED
EXACTLY
WHEN
I WAS
LEAVING THEM.

Ashleigh
Brilliant

IF
YOU DON'T
BELIEVE IN
GHOSTS,

YOU'VE NEVER
BEEN TO
A FAMILY
REUNION.

Ashleigh
Brilliant

It seems like only yesterday that we were calling Today Tomorrow.

Ashleigh Brilliant

I DIDN'T
REALIZE
HOW MUCH
THE WORLD
WAS
CHANGING,

UNTIL
I LOOKED
IN THE
MIRROR.

Ashleigh Brilliant

ONE
REQUIREMENT
FOR STAYING
COMPLETELY
HEALTHY
UNTIL YOU DIE

IS
TO DIE
VERY
SUDDENLY.

Ashleigh Brilliant

All Change 127

Ashleigh Brilliant

WILL YOU STILL LOVE ME,

WHEN I'M NO LONGER SO LOVABLE?

LIFE BECOMES MUCH EASIER,

ONCE YOU GET THROUGH YOUTH, MIDDLE AGE, AND OLD AGE.

Ashleigh Brilliant

BABIES CAN BE MADE IN A FEW MONTHS,

BUT IT TAKES SEVENTY YEARS TO MAKE A SEVENTY-YEAR-OLD.

Ashleigh Brilliant

MY STRANGE
BEHAVIOR
AS A CHILD
IS EASILY
EXPLAINED:

I WAS TRAINING
TO BECOME
A STRANGE ADULT.

Ashleigh Brilliant

I'LL
FEEL
BETTER
WHEN
I'VE HAD
A GOOD
LIFE.

Ashleigh Brilliant

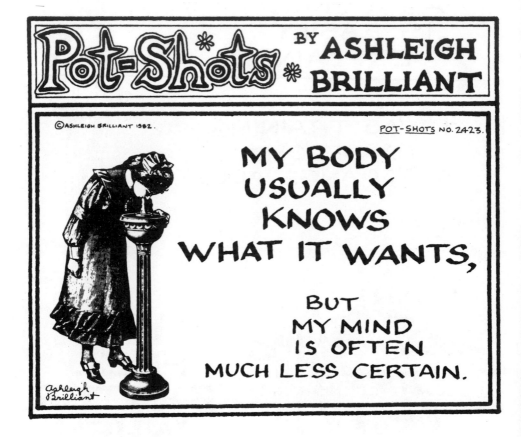

Pot-Shots BY ASHLEIGH BRILLIANT

© ASHLEIGH BRILLIANT 1982.

POT-SHOTS NO. 2423.

MY BODY
USUALLY
KNOWS
WHAT IT WANTS,

BUT
MY MIND
IS OFTEN
MUCH LESS CERTAIN.

X. What the Health

For those of us whose personal property happens to include anything as valuable as a mind and a body, the question of proper maintenance is necessarily of some concern. Various types of diseases have been in vogue at different times, but, with the modern shift of emphasis from healing to prevention, and with dieting, fasting, and other forms of self-denial becoming increasingly fashionable, more and more of us are being encouraged to do without illness altogether, if we possibly can. It's true that this could create something of a hardship in various illness-dependent trades and professions; but, so far, the Undertaking Industry does not even seem to be taking the threat seriously—and we are no doubt still a long way from being required by our government, for the sake of the economy, to maintain a certain minimum level of sickness.

Some people, however, still do occasionally encounter severe shortages of good health. One of my more fervent followers has actually been attempting to improve the condition of certain elderly invalids by administering a carefully-measured dose of one Pot-Shot per day. Unfortunately, the results of this purportedly "controlled" experiment have been inconclusive, at least partly because the kind-hearted experimenter, after failing (not surprisingly!) to devise any satisfactory placebo, could not bring himself to inflict *Pot-Shot* deprivation upon his intended "control-group."

POT-SHOTS NO. 2655.

ALWAYS TAKE YOUR VITAMINS IN ALPHABETICAL ORDER:

IT HASN'T YET BEEN PROVEN NECESSARY, BUT WHY TAKE CHANCES?

© ASHLEIGH BRILLIANT 1982.

Ashleigh Brilliant

NO SENSE DYING BEFORE LUNCH

© BRILLIANT ENTERPRISES 1968   *Ashleigh Brilliant*

POT- SHOTS NO. 72

THE DOCTORS HAVE BEEN DOING EVERYTHING IN THEIR POWER,

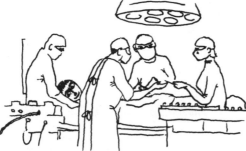

BUT SOMEHOW, I AM STILL ALIVE.

IF COFFEE DIDN'T EXIST,

SOMEBODY WOULD HAVE TO INVENT IT FOR ME VERY SOON.

POT-SHOTS NO. 2871.

HOW CAN I CONCENTRATE ON BEING ILL,

IF PEOPLE KEEP TRYING TO MAKE ME WELL?

Ashleigh Brilliant

POT-SHOTS NO. 3076.

MY MIND IS RESTING ~

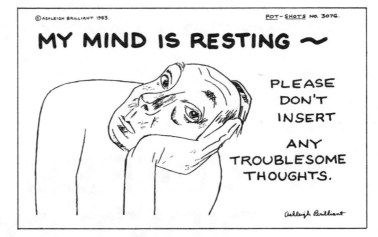

PLEASE DON'T INSERT

ANY TROUBLESOME THOUGHTS.

Ashleigh Brilliant

POT-SHOTS NO. 2719.

FREQUENT EXERTION

IS ONE WAY TO PREVENT THE PAINS CAUSED BY INFREQUENT EXERTION.

Ashleigh Brilliant

DECIDING I'M GUILTY IS EASY ~

WHAT'S HARD IS
DECIDING
THE LENGTH
AND SEVERITY
OF MY
PUNISHMENT.

Ashleigh Brilliant

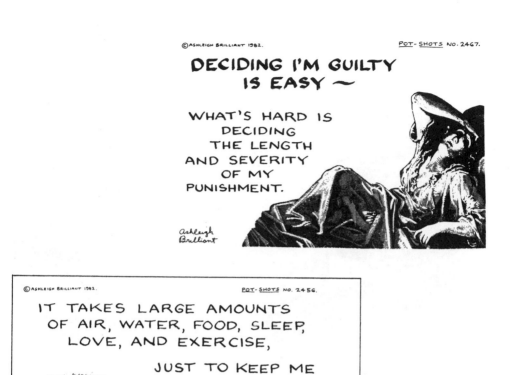

IT TAKES LARGE AMOUNTS
OF AIR, WATER, FOOD, SLEEP,
LOVE, AND EXERCISE,

JUST TO KEEP ME
WORRYING.

Ashleigh Brilliant

WITH
PSYCHIATRIC
HELP
SO EXPENSIVE
AND
TIME-CONSUMING,
I CAN'T AFFORD
TO BE
MORE THAN
SLIGHTLY
UNHAPPY.

Ashleigh Brilliant

What the Health 135

IF ONLY I COULD LEARN TO LIVE HAPPILY WITHOUT EVERYTHING THAT SEEMS TO MAKE LIFE WORTH LIVING.

Ashleigh Brilliant

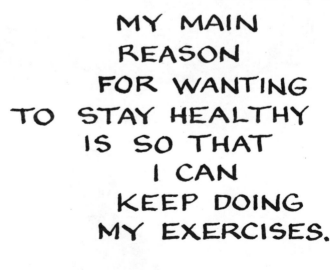

MY MAIN REASON FOR WANTING TO STAY HEALTHY IS SO THAT I CAN KEEP DOING MY EXERCISES.

Ashleigh Brilliant

POT-SHOTS NO. 2371.

MANY THINGS ARE GOOD FOR DEPRESSION,

BUT
I DON'T
KNOW
ANYTHING
THAT DEPRESSION
IS GOOD FOR.

Ashleigh Brilliant

POT-SHOTS NO. 2471.

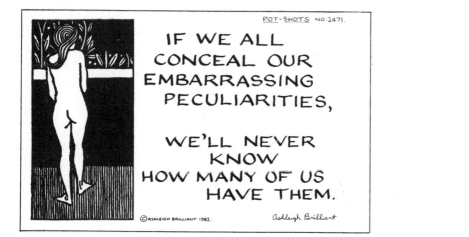

IF WE ALL
CONCEAL OUR
EMBARRASSING
PECULIARITIES,

WE'LL NEVER
KNOW
HOW MANY OF US
HAVE THEM.

Ashleigh Brilliant

POT-SHOTS NO. 2485.

Ashleigh Brilliant

TIME IS
RUNNING OUT,

AND
I HAVEN'T YET
GOT ALL MY
WORRYING
DONE.

What the Health 137

POT-SHOTS NO. 2609.

I'm afraid there may be something about myself that I'm allergic to.

Ashleigh Brilliant

POT-SHOTS NO. 749.

MEET ME HALF-WAY:

YOU NEED THE EXERCISE.

Ashleigh Brilliant

POT-SHOTS NO. 3105.

INSTEAD OF PAST, PRESENT, AND FUTURE,

I'D PREFER CHOCOLATE, VANILLA, AND STRAWBERRY.

Ashleigh Brilliant

POT-SHOTS NO. 2491.

© ASHLEIGH BRILLIANT 1982.

THERE WAS NEVER ANY INSANITY IN MY FAMILY,

UNTIL I GOT MARRIED.

Ashleigh Brilliant

POT-SHOTS NO. 786.

DON'T GET WELL TOO SOON

YOUR SUFFERING IS AN INSPIRATION TO US ALL.

Ashleigh Brilliant

© BRILLIANT ENTERPRISES 1975.

© ASHLEIGH BRILLIANT 1983.

POT-SHOTS NO. 2858.

IT COSTS MONEY TO STAY HEALTHY,

BUT IT'S EVEN MORE EXPENSIVE TO GET SICK.

Ashleigh Brilliant

What the Health 139

POT-SHOTS NO. 2983.

IT'S TOO LATE
IN THE DAY
TO RELAX—

I'LL
HAVE TO GO
STRAIGHT
TO BED.

© ASHLEIGH BRILLIANT 1983.

© BRILLIANT ENTERPRISES 1975.

POT-SHOTS NO. 737

I MAY NOT
BE PROSPEROUS,
BUT
AT LEAST I'M
OVERWEIGHT.

© ASHLEIGH BRILLIANT 1982.

POT-SHOTS NO. 2671.

IF
IT'S
SWEET,

IT WANTS
ME
TO EAT IT.

140

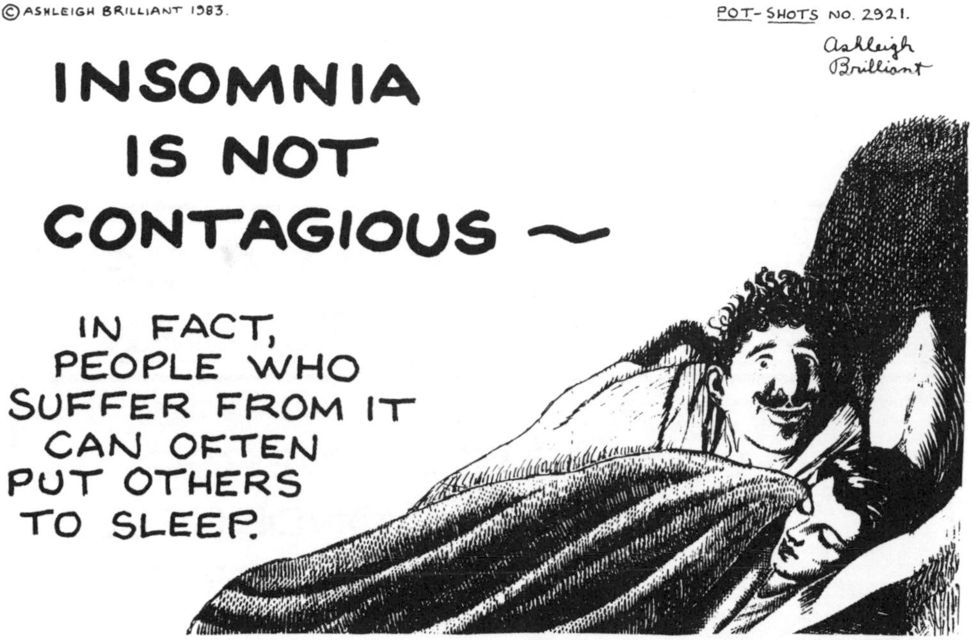

©ASHLEIGH BRILLIANT 1983.
POT-SHOTS NO. 2921.
Ashleigh Brilliant
INSOMNIA IS NOT CONTAGIOUS ~
IN FACT, PEOPLE WHO SUFFER FROM IT CAN OFTEN PUT OTHERS TO SLEEP.

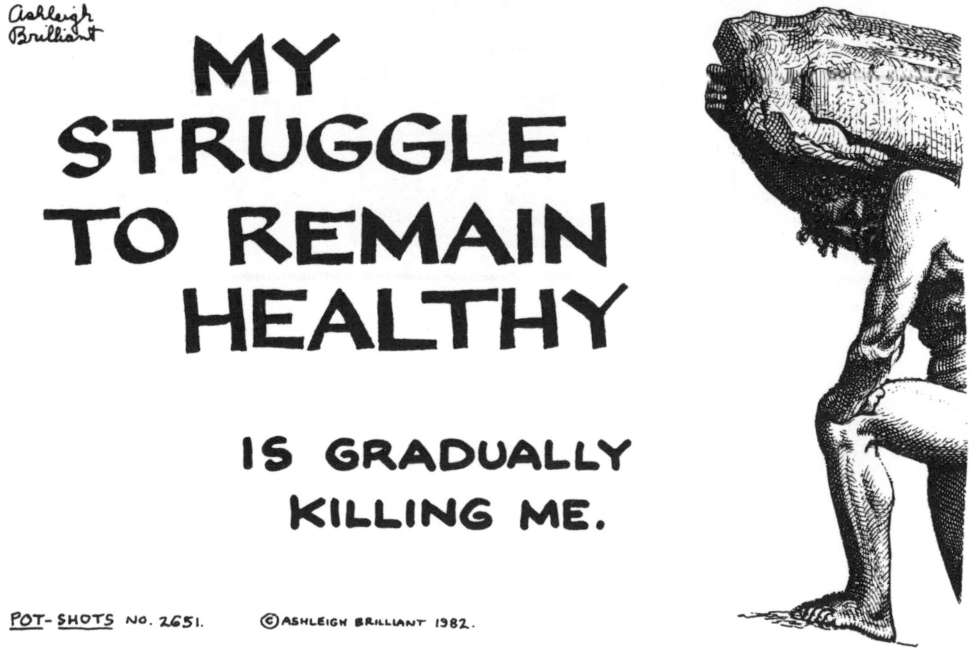

Ashleigh Brilliant
MY STRUGGLE TO REMAIN HEALTHY
IS GRADUALLY KILLING ME.
POT-SHOTS NO. 2651.
©ASHLEIGH BRILLIANT 1982.

XI. Questioning the Answers

When it comes (as it does in this section) to matters religious and philosophical, delicate measuring instruments have determined that the shortest distance between two points of any argument is exactly the length of one Brilliant Thought. And why not? After all, is there any idea worthy of serious consideration in these busy times which cannot be fully expressed in seventeen words or less?

Surely there is just as much need now as ever for Wisdom in the world; but people, quite understandably, no longer have the time or the patience to go on long and arduous quests in search of it. They prefer it to arrive in some neat, concise format in the daily paper, or with the day's mail. If they can find it on a T-shirt, a drinking-mug, or any other object requiring not even the scanning of a page, so much the better.

Seizing this opportunity, I have gone into the Wisdom Business, and shamelessly play the game of "Licensing," hiring out my Thoughts to appear in newspapers, and on a wide variety of other commercial surfaces. Who would have thought that Wisdom could ever be marketed so successfully? The secret is, of course, in having a dependable supply of this increasingly rare commodity. What is my source?—a remote mine I happened to stumble upon one day, after years of prospecting—hidden between my ears.

TAKE CARE OF WHAT YOU LOVE,

AND TRY TO LOVE WHATEVER YOU HAVE TO TAKE CARE OF.

Ashleigh Brilliant

Is it better
to leave life
still wanting more,

or satisfied
that you've
had enough?

Ashleigh Brilliant

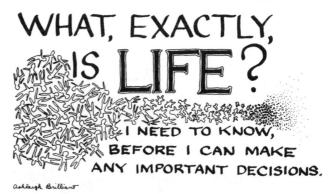

WHAT, EXACTLY, IS LIFE?

I NEED TO KNOW, BEFORE I CAN MAKE ANY IMPORTANT DECISIONS.

Ashleigh Brilliant

FOR FURTHER INFORMATION,

CONSULT GOD.

Ashleigh Brilliant

So many impossibilities turn out to be true, it might be safer if we all believed everything.

Ashleigh Brilliant

Questioning the Answers 145

DON'T LET THEM DESTROY THE HYPOCRISY OF CHRISTMAS ～

IT'S THE ONLY PART I ENJOY.

Ashleigh Brilliant

THAT MUST BE THE ANSWER—

GOD IS A COMMITTEE.

Ashleigh Brilliant

LIFE IS PART OF A GREAT ADVENTURE I'M HAVING.

Ashleigh Brilliant

AS SOON AS
EVERYBODY CHOOSES
THE WRONG SIDE,

IT THEN,
BY SOME MIRACLE,
BECOMES
THE RIGHT SIDE.

Ashleigh
Brilliant

© ASHLEIGH BRILLIANT 1983.

AREN'T
I LUCKY,

TO HAVE
SURVIVED

SO MUCH
BAD LUCK.

Ashleigh
Brilliant

POT-SHOTS NO. 2434.

IF ONLY I COULD ALWAYS HAVE

A GOOD REPUTATION,

WITHOUT ALWAYS HAVING TO BE GOOD.

Ashleigh Brilliant

POT-SHOTS NO. 2387.

THE FUTURE MAY CONSIDER ME WRONG,

BUT THE FUTURE WON'T NECESSARILY BE RIGHT.

Ashleigh Brilliant

POT-
SHOTS
NO. 2368.

IT'S NOT THAT I'M AN ATHEIST,

BUT RATHER
THAT I'M
A MEMBER OF
GOD'S
LOYAL
OPPOSITION.

Ashleigh
Brilliant

POT-SHOTS NO. 2991.

UNDERSTANDING THE WORLD IS NOT MY WHOLE PROBLEM~

ANOTHER
PART IS:
MAKING
THE WORLD
UNDERSTAND
ME.

Ashleigh
Brilliant

IF ONLY I COULD
SEE MYSELF
IN MY
PROPER
PERSPECTIVE.

Ashleigh
Brilliant

I'M ACTUALLY VERY RELIGIOUS --
DO YOU HAVE ANYTHING I CAN WORSHIP?

Ashleigh
Brilliant

IN THE
CONTINUING
WAR
BETWEEN
GOOD
AND
EVIL,

THOSE OF US
WITH ANY SENSE
WILL REMAIN
NEUTRAL.

Ashleigh Brilliant

POT-SHOTS NO. 2703.

IF I EVER BECOME A SAINT,

IT WILL BE A MIRACLE.

Ashleigh Brilliant

POT-SHOTS NO. 2791.

BY WHAT RIGHT DO I HOLD THE POWER OF LIFE AND DEATH OVER MYSELF?

Ashleigh Brilliant

Ashleigh Brilliant

WHEN I'M SURE I'M RIGHT, NOTHING CAN STOP ME ~

BUT I'M NEVER THAT SURE.

How can I do what's expected of me, if nobody ever expects anything of me?

Ashleigh Brilliant

I'VE SEEN BETTER DAYS, AND WORSE DAYS,

BUT THIS IS THE ONLY DAY I'LL SEE TODAY.

Ashleigh Brilliant

DON'T DO WHAT YOU SHOULDN'T

unless there's a very good reason why you should.

Ashleigh Brilliant

GOD MAY CLAIM TO HAVE CREATED THE WORLD,

BUT CAN HE PRODUCE ANY WITNESSES?

Ashleigh Brilliant

AFTER COMING THIS FAR IN LIFE, I MIGHT AS WELL GO ALL THE WAY.

Ashleigh Brilliant

Questioning the Answers 153

Pot-Shots BY ASHLEIGH BRILLIANT

POT-SHOTS NO. 2402.

I'VE EXPLORED
AND REJECTED
EVERY OTHER
POSSIBILITY ~

LIFE,
AFTER ALL,
MUST BE
FOR HAVING
FUN.

Ashleigh Brilliant

XII. A Cheerful Earful

Here we are, at the last chapter, and, as your reward (or penalty) for staying with me this far, I have saved for you a careless (if not quite carefree) collection of dubiously inspiring and consoling messages, including some of the most half-heartedly cheerful sentiments ever extracted from a single over-burdened mind.

Of course, I am well aware how careful one must be when it comes to dispensing cheer. If enough of us were to stay cheerful enough for long enough, it could endanger some of our most cherished institutions, and indeed threaten our entire way of life. Nevertheless, an occasional small piece of attenuated Joy, taken under supervised conditions, need be no more psychologically disturbing than the average newspaper headline or family gathering.

I therefore make no apologies for hoping to leave you feeling at least no worse than I found you. Such little scraps of encouragement as I can offer may be totally worthless. But these are difficult times, and, if you are anything like me, you need all the worthless encouragement you can get.

Your Smile is one of the great sights of the world.

Ashleigh Brilliant

POT-SHOTS NO. 301

BE BRAVE

REMEMBER:
THE WORST
THAT CAN HAPPEN IS
THE WORST THAT CAN HAPPEN.

THERE'S A BETTER TIME COMING ~

OR DID WE MISS IT IN THE NIGHT?

CONSIDERING HOW ISOLATED THE EARTH IS, WE'RE LUCKY IT HAS SO MANY OF THE THINGS WE NEED.

POT-SHOTS No. 2980.

I ORDER YOU TO BE HAPPY!

THE PENALTY FOR DISOBEDIENCE IS: UNHAPPINESS.

POT-SHOTS NO. 842.

LET'S BE PROUD OF WHAT WE ARE,

REGARDLESS OF THE FACTS.

Ashleigh Brilliant

POT-SHOTS NO. 2796.

Ashleigh Brilliant

KEEP TAKING CHANCES

THIS COULD BE YOUR LUCKY LIFE!

POT-SHOTS NO. 2548

Ashleigh Brilliant

PERSEVERE!

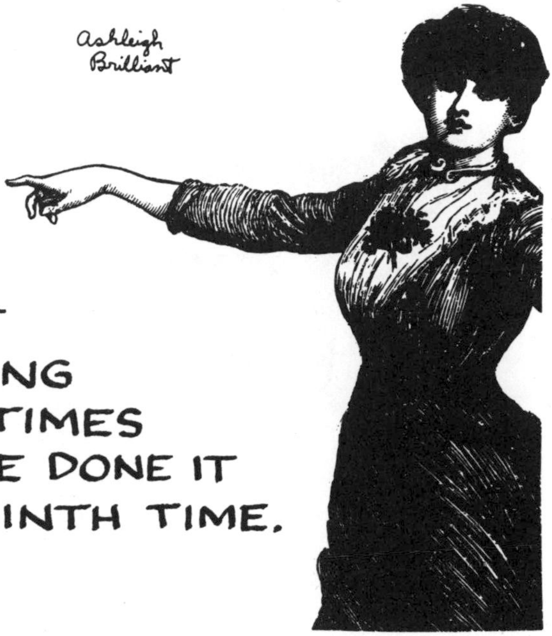

YOU CAN'T
DO ANYTHING
A HUNDRED TIMES
BEFORE YOU'VE DONE IT
THE NINETY-NINTH TIME.

POT-SHOTS NO. 2787.

DON'T WORRY!
IF YOU KEEP
PUTTING OFF DECISIONS,
EVENTUALLY
THEY'LL ALL
BE MADE FOR YOU.

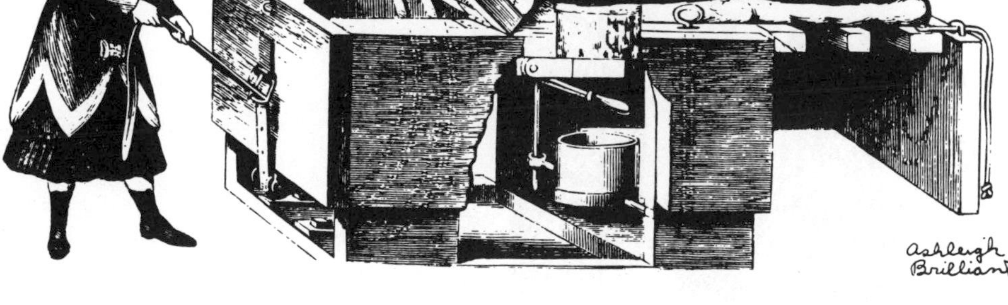

Ashleigh Brilliant

© ASHLEIGH BRILLIANT 1983.   POT-SHOTS NO. 3114.

YOU AND I
NEVER KNEW
HOW
WONDERFUL
WE WERE

BEFORE
WE MET
EACH OTHER.

Ashleigh Brilliant

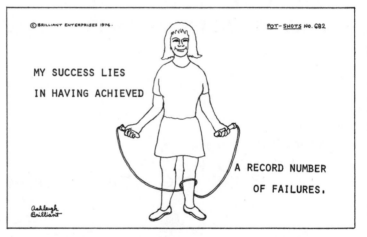

© BRILLIANT ENTERPRISES 1974.   POT-SHOTS NO. GB2

MY SUCCESS LIES

IN HAVING ACHIEVED

A RECORD NUMBER

OF FAILURES.

Ashleigh Brilliant

POT-SHOTS NO. 2675.

© ASHLEIGH BRILLIANT 1982.

FROM
ALL
OF
US

TO ALL
OF
YOU,

THIS
EMPTY
GREETING.

Ashleigh Brilliant

Ashleigh
Brilliant

THERE'S NO HARM IN TALKING TO YOURSELF,

BUT
TRY TO
AVOID
TELLING
YOURSELF
JOKES
YOU'VE
HEARD BEFORE.

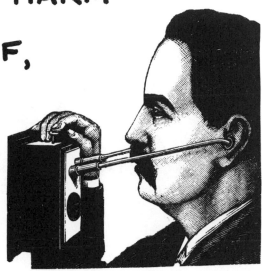

Ashleigh
Brilliant

KEEP SMILING!

(BUT NOT
SO MUCH
THAT PEOPLE
BEGIN TO WONDER
IF YOU ARE
MENTALLY
UNBALANCED.)

A Cheerful Earful 161

Ashleigh Brilliant

IN SOME CASES,
A BROKEN HEART
PROVES
TO BE
ONLY A
SUPERFICIAL
WOUND.

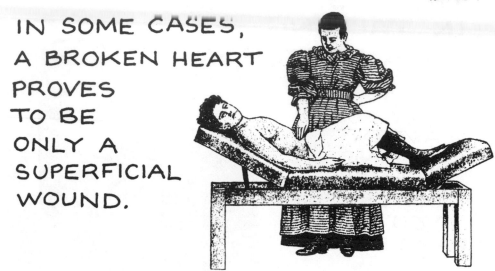

MOUNTAINS
MAKE GOOD FRIENDS ~

THEY'LL
WAIT
PATIENTLY,

EVEN IF
YOU
GO AWAY
FOR YEARS.

Ashleigh Brilliant

POT-SHOTS No. 559

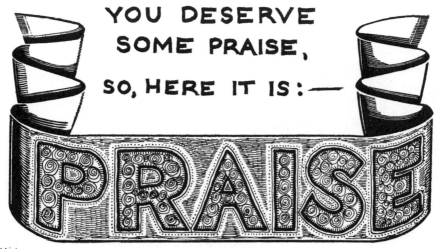

YOU DESERVE SOME PRAISE, SO, HERE IT IS:—

PRAISE

Ashleigh Brilliant

POT-SHOTS No. 3115.

NO MATTER HOW FAR YOU GO FROM ME ~ YOU CAN NEVER PASS THE POINT OF NO RETURN.

Ashleigh Brilliant

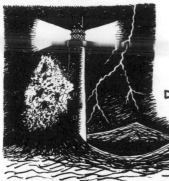

TRY NOT TO
DESPAIR—
THESE ARE
DIFFICULT TIMES
FOR GOD, TOO.

Ashleigh Brilliant

I BELIEVE
I CAN LIVE
ANOTHER 100 YEARS,

BUT
IT'LL TAKE ME
100 YEARS
TO PROVE IT.

Ashleigh Brilliant

Ashleigh Brilliant

THERE ARE NO
IMPORTANT DIFFERENCES
BETWEEN MEN AND WOMEN

BUT THE
UNIMPORTANT ONES
ARE SOMETIMES
VERY INTERESTING.

IN A DEMOCRACY,

EVERY LITTLE WRONG IDEA MAY GROW UP TO BECOME NATIONAL POLICY.

Ashleigh Brilliant

MARRIAGE STILL CONFERS ONE VERY SPECIAL PRIVILEGE:

ONLY A MARRIED PERSON CAN GET DIVORCED.

Ashleigh Brilliant

IN MANY WAYS, THE WORLD'S IMPROVED IN MY TIME,

BUT
I DON'T
NECESSARILY
DESERVE
ALL THE CREDIT.

Ashleigh
Brilliant

Ashleigh
Brilliant

TRY TO LIVE FOREVER

YOU MAY
NOT SUCCEED,
BUT
IT'S WORTH
THE EFFORT.

I Hate To Say Goodbye,

(So I Won't)*

The book stops here. At least, this is where I have to stop writing it, although you (lucky you!) can go back and read it over and over, possibly getting even more out of it than I ever realized I was putting into it.

But the really good news is that this is not all there is. There are thousands more Brilliant Thoughts waiting for you on individual postcards, in books, and in many other exciting and useful forms. Better yet, all this is within almost ridiculously easy reach, through the magic of a most unusual mail-order system, which I personally invented, and which since 1967 has been happily filling the needs of all kinds of readers, in many parts of the world. For both our sakes, I hope you'll want to continue our relationship, by sending for my Catalogue, which includes many Brilliant messages unobtainable anywhere else, and comes with sample postcards and a handsome order form, enabling you to choose the exact messages most appropriate for your own special purposes. The current (1992) price is two U.S. dollars. Please enclose that amount, or its equivalent, in your own time and currency. My address is:

Ashleigh Brilliant
117 W. Valerio St.
Santa Barbara, California 93101, U.S.A.

Pot Shot No. 112